PAINTING PROJECTS

7

Sammie Crawford

decorating chairs

4880 Lower Valley Road • Atglen, PA 19310

Other Schiffer Books by the Author:
Holiday Fun: Painting Christmas Gourds
978-0-7643-3279-1, $14.99

Painting Gourds with the Fairy Gourdmother®
978-0-7643-4309-4, $16.99

Time for Gourds: 8 Clock Projects
978-0-7643-3981-3, $16.99

Gourd Fun for Everyone
978-0-7643-3124-4, $22.99

Building Gourd Birdhouses with the Fairy Gourdmother®
978-0-7643-3736-9, $24.99

Creating Gourd Birds with the Fairy Gourdmother®
978-0-7643-3735-2, $24.99

Making Gourd Bowls with the Fairy Gourdmother®
978-0-7643-3980-6, $16.99

Other Schiffer Books on Related Subjects:
Cane & Rush Seating, 978-0-7643-4547-0, $24.99

Copyright © 2014 by Sammie Crawford

Library of Congress Control Number: 2014946283

All rights reserved. No part of this work may be reproduced or used in any form or by any means—graphic, electronic, or mechanical, including photocopying or information storage and retrieval systems—without written permission from the publisher.

The scanning, uploading, and distribution of this book or any part thereof via the Internet or via any other means without the permission of the publisher is illegal and punishable by law. Please purchase only authorized editions and do not participate in or encourage the electronic piracy of copyrighted materials.
"Schiffer," "Schiffer Publishing, Ltd. & Design," and the "Design of pen and inkwell" are registered trademarks of Schiffer Publishing, Ltd.

Designed by RoS
Type set in Swiss924 BT/Humanst521 BT

ISBN: 978-0-7643-4773-3
Printed in China

Published by Schiffer Publishing, Ltd.
4880 Lower Valley Road
Atglen, PA 19310
Phone: (610) 593-1777; Fax: (610) 593-2002
E-mail: Info@schifferbooks.com

For our complete selection of fine books on this and related subjects, please visit our website at www.schifferbooks.com. You may also write for a free catalog.

This book may be purchased from the publisher. Please try your bookstore first.

We are always looking for people to write books on new and related subjects. If you have an idea for a book, please contact us at proposals@schifferbooks.com.

Schiffer Publishing's titles are available at special discounts for bulk purchases for sales promotions or premiums. Special editions, including personalized covers, corporate imprints, and excerpts can be created in large quantities for special needs. For more information, contact the publisher.

Contents

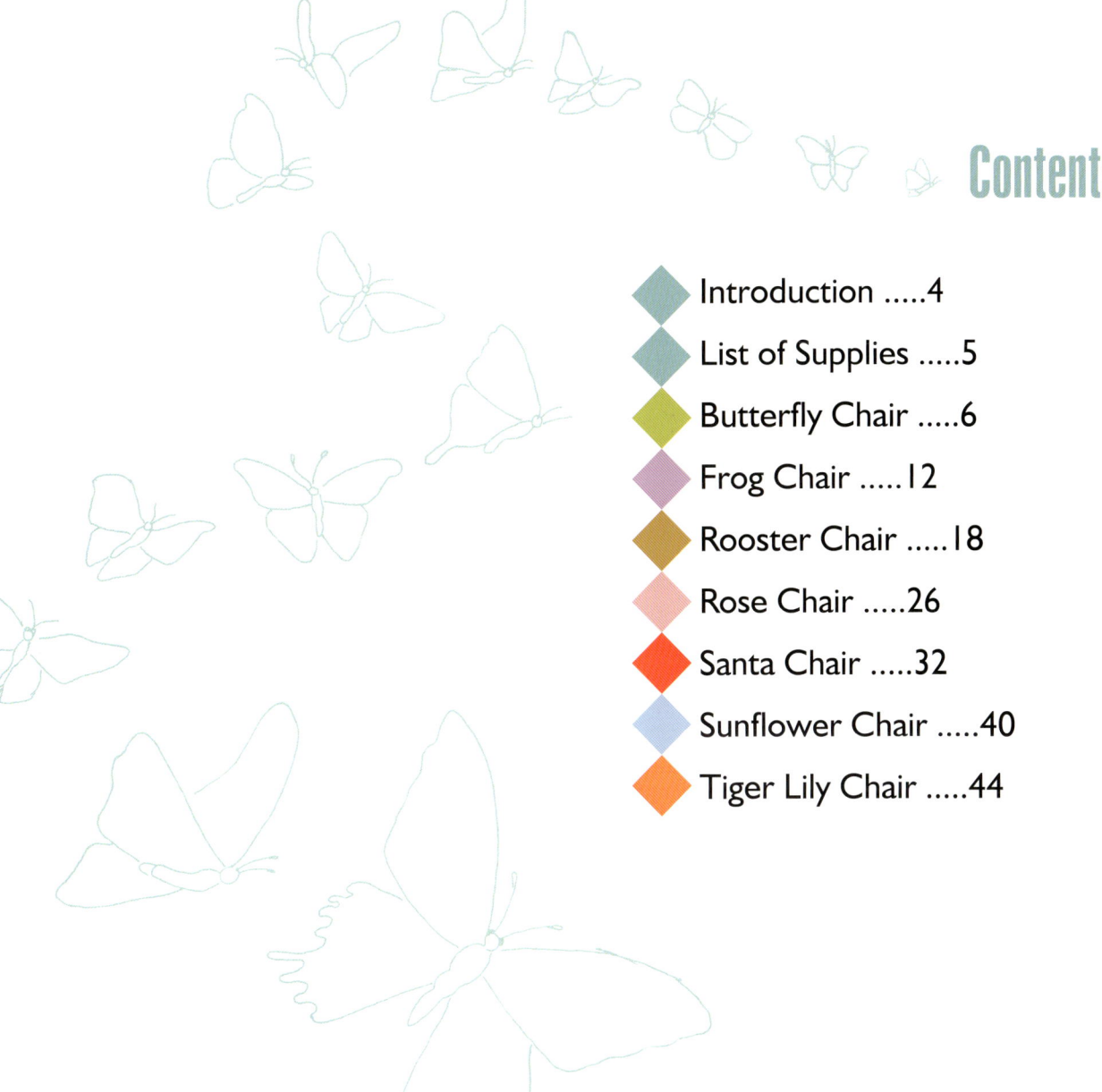

◆ Introduction 4
◆ List of Supplies 5
◆ Butterfly Chair 6
◆ Frog Chair 12
◆ Rooster Chair 18
◆ Rose Chair 26
◆ Santa Chair 32
◆ Sunflower Chair 40
◆ Tiger Lily Chair 44

Introduction

After painting two children's chairs for a friend, I decided to paint a chair that had been in the garage for about twenty years. Little did I know that it would lead to more and more — sort of like eating one peanut! Since then, I have totally exhausted the supply of used chairs in this town and have had to branch out to surrounding areas.

If you are a good bargain finder, you shouldn't have to pay more than $10 for a used chair, but you should be ready to do some repair work on it. Some only need a little glue or wood filler, but some are major undertakings, like the three-legged chair someone gave me — that one was a total rebuild — and I can't thank my husband enough for his talents and his patience. It reached the point where he would groan every time he saw me pull in and lift the hatch on the car.

I donated several of the chairs to my painting club to auction off as a fund-raiser, but my studio soon became overrun with chairs. I kept on painting and, before I knew it, I had enough to do a book. I hope you enjoy it and gain ideas for painting and decorating your own used chairs.

about the author

Sammie Crawford has enjoyed multiple careers, but her favorite pursuit since childhood has been art. She teaches decorative painting, and is well-known for her gourd art. Some of her gourd ornaments have hung on the White House Christmas Tree and are in the Smithsonian Collection. She has published nine books. She lives in Hot Springs, Arkansas, with her high school sweetheart and husband of 48 years.

List of Supplies

You should have on hand the standard supplies for painting these chairs:

- Tracing paper
- Transfer paper
- Stylus
- White and grey chalk pencils
- Q-tips® or cotton swabs
- Paper towels
- Palette paper
- Blending gel
- Spray varnish
- Assorted brushes

All the chairs received several light coats of varnish when they were completed. You may use matte if you prefer, but I used gloss. It gives a better finish.

Palette — DecoArt

- Olive Green
- Charcoal
- Orchid
- Moon Yellow
- Bluegrass
- Spiced Pumpkin
- Winter Blue
- White
- Cinnamon Drop
- True Ochre
- Georgia Clay
- Dove
- Dioxazine Purple
- Black
- Neutral Grey

Brushes — Loew-Cornell

- Series 7300 # 12 flat
- Series 7350 10/0 liner
- Series 7550 1" wash
- #275 1/2" mop

Supplies

- Thrift store chair
- Sandpaper
- White spray paint
- 1/4" Masonite or plywood
- Craft saw
- Staple gun
- Gloss spray varnish
- Blending gel

BUTTERFLY chair

Preparing the Chair

1. Make any needed repairs and spray the chair White.
2. Cut the large butterfly from Masonite.
3. Sand any rough edges.

Painting the Design

1. **The Largest Butterfly** on the seat and the one on the back are the same: Basecoat it Olive Green on the top wings; apply Charcoal to lower portion of the upper wing and drag the mop through it into the green area. This will give a blended edge. Do the same with the bars on the wings. Shade veins in the charcoal section with Black and with Charcoal on other sections. Float around the body with Neutral Grey.

1a. **On the Lower Wing**, apply swatches of Moon Yellow, Orchid, Spiced Pumpkin, Winter Blue, and Bluegrass side by side. Apply Charcoal to the rest of the wing and drag the mop through it into the other colors.

2. **Second Butterfly** – Moon, Charcoal, and Winter Blue
3. **Third Butterfly** – Moon, Charcoal, and True Ochre
4. **Fourth Butterfly** – Moon, Spiced Pumpkin, and Georgia Clay
5. **Fifth Butterfly** – Moon, Winter Blue, and Black
6. **Sixth Butterfly** – Black, White, Georgia Clay, and Dove Grey
7. **Seventh Butterfly** – Winter Blue, Spiced Pumpkin, Black and White
8. **Eighth Butterfly** – Spiced Pumpkin, Black, and White
9. **Ninth Butterfly** – Black and White
10. **Tenth Butterfly** – Orchid, Dioxazine Purple, Black, and White
11. **Eleventh Butterfly** – Winter Blue, White, Charcoal and Spiced Pumpkin
12. **Twelfth Butterfly** – Moon and Black
13. **Thirteenth Butterfly** – Spiced Pumpkin, White, and Charcoal
14. **All Bodies** are Charcoal.
15. **The Rainbow** is Cinnamon Drop, Orchid, Moon Yellow, Winter Blue, and Bluegrass in that order. Apply blending gel to the area to help move the colors around as needed.

butterfly chair back

flip pattern for other side

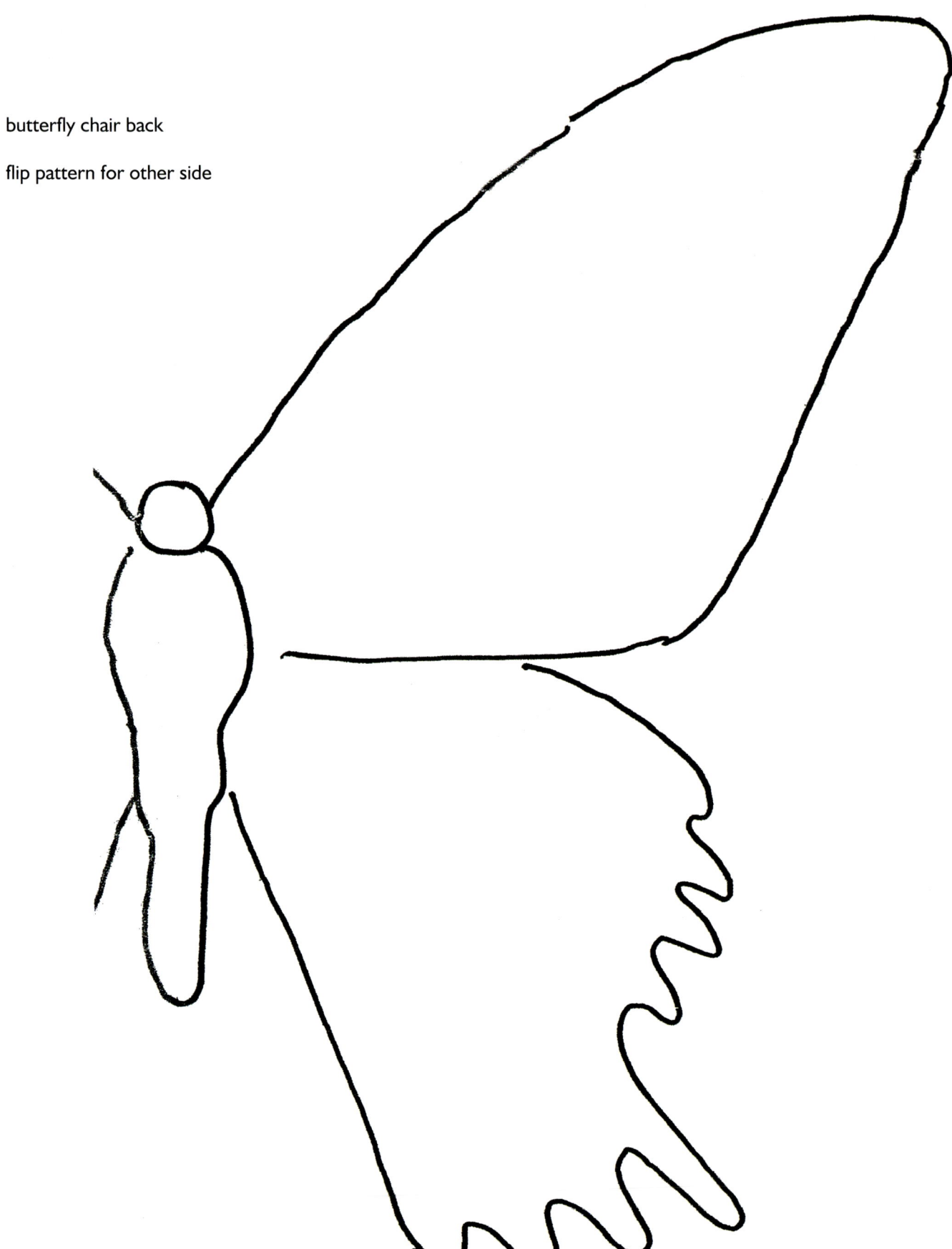

butterfly chair seat

Palette — DecoArt

- Olive Green
- Hauser Dark Green
- White
- Soft Sage
- Antique White
- Black
- Lt. Buttermilk
- Golden Straw
- Lemon
- Spiced Pumpkin
- True Red
- Orchid
- Lilac
- Pansy Lavender
- Rookwood Red

Brushes — Loew-Cornell

- Series 7300 # 12 flat
- Series 7350 10/0 liner
- Series 7500 # 4 filbert

Supplies

- Thrift store chair
- White spray paint
- Sandpaper
- Wood glue
- 1/4" plywood or Masonite
- Craft saw
- Gloss spray varnish

Preparing the Chair

1. Make any needed repairs and spray paint the chair White.

2. Apply the outline for the frog and orchid to the plywood and cut out.

3. Sand any rough edges and paint it White.

4. Apply the pattern minus details and basecoat the frog Olive Green and the flower Orchid.

Painting the Design

1. **Frog** – Paint the tummy Light Buttermilk and float it where it meets the Olive Green. Shade it with Antique White. The toes are Golden Straw. Shade the frog using HDG and hi-lite with Soft Sage.

2. **Eyes** – Base with Spiced Pumpkin. Float True Red around the edges, fading inward. Paint the pupils Black and add a White comma stroke for hi-lite. On the side opposite the hi-lite, float a Rookwood Red "c" stroke on the red portion of the eyes against the edge, fading inward. Outline the iris with a very thin line of Lemon. Outline the entire eye with a thin line of Soft Sage.

3. **Palm** – Basecoat with Avocado, shade with Evergreen, and hi-lite with Celery.

4. **Orchid** – Shade the flower with Pansy Lavender and hi-lite with Lilac. The stamens are Antique White with Golden Straw ends.

frog chair seat

frog chair back

Palette — DecoArt

Antique White
Asphaltum
Cocoa
Soft Black
Spiced Pumpkin
White
Burnt Orange
Orange Twist
Black
Spicy Mustard
Yellow Ochre
Sand
Raw Sienna
Crimson Tide
Khaki
Black Plum
Honey
Mississippi Mud
Cadmium Orange
Rookwood Red
Hauser Dark Green

Traditions Paints

Phthalo Green
Opaque White

Brushes — Loew-Cornell

Series 7300 # 12 flat shader
Series 7350 10/0 liner
Series 7520 ½" filbert rake
Series 7550 1" wash
275 1/2" mop

Supplies

Thrift store chair
White spray paint
3/8" plywood
Craft saw
Sandpaper
Gloss spray varnish

Preparing the Chair

1. Make any needed repairs.

2. Spray-paint the chair White.

3. Cut the chicken out of plywood and sand any rough edges.

Painting the Design

1. Paint the top of the chair Orange Twist.

2. Paint the legs Crimson Tide, Yellow Ochre, and Hauser Dark Green (refer to the photograph).

3. Apply pattern and shade around the chickens on back of chair with Raw Sienna.

4. Apply pattern to the seat and paint the chicken wire using the liner brush and Soft Black.

5. Apply basic lines of the pattern on the chicken cut-out and basecoat as follows:
   a. **Head and Neck** – Spiced Pumpkin on the left side, Spicy Mustard on the right
   b. **Breast** – Antique White
   c. **Tail** – White undercoat, then Phthalo Green
   d. **Beak and Feet** – Yellow Ochre
   e. **Ground** – Khaki
   f. **Comb** – Crimson Tide
   g. **Saddle feathers** – Spiced Pumpkin

6. Shade the head and neck with Burnt Orange on left and Honey on the right.

7. Float Soft Black on the tips of some of the feathers.

8. The veins are Antique White.

9. Wash the upper area around the wattle with Spiced Pumpkin.

10. Shade the comb with Black Plum and hi-lite with Cadmium Orange.

11. Shade the beak with Raw Sienna and hi-lite with Sand.

12. Shade the saddle with Burnt Orange and hi-lite with Orange Twist.

13. Paint the veins Orange Twist using the liner brush.

14. Wash the saddle next to the Spicy Mustard feathers with Rookwood Red to deepen the shadows.

15. Shade around the breast feathers with Cocoa.

16. Float "c" strokes on the feathers with Asphaltum.

17. Paint the veins Antique White.

18. Float a Soft Black wash on the lower body near the tail feathers.

19. Shade the tail feathers with Black.

20. Hi-lite with a mix of Phthalo Green and Opaque White 3:1.

21. Use the liner brush to pull Phthalo veins and radiating lines along the veins.

22. Shade the ground with Mississippi Mud.

23. Shade the feet the same as the beak with Soft Black claws.

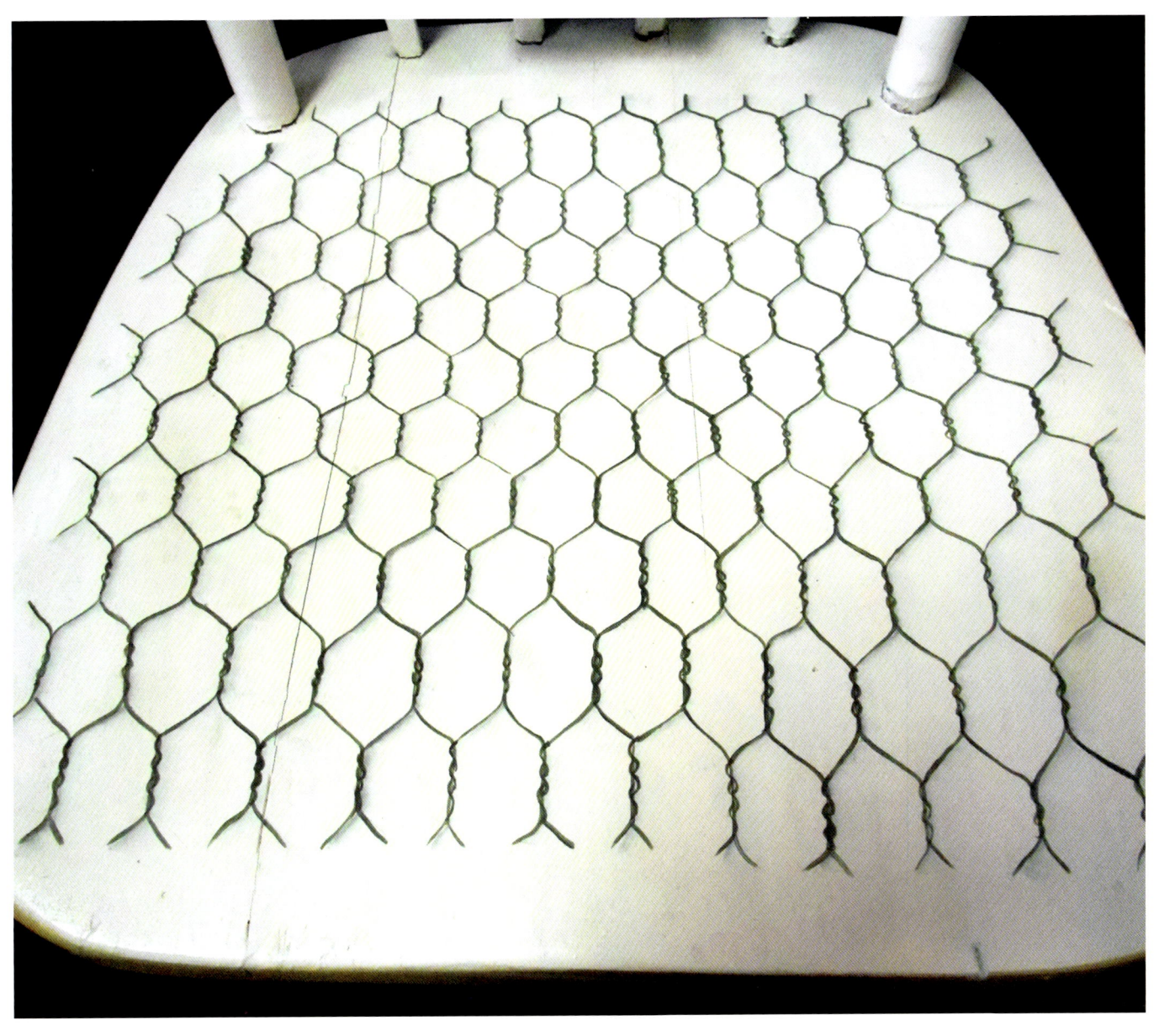

Note: the "connectors" are just three "S's."
Repeat as needed to cover chair seat

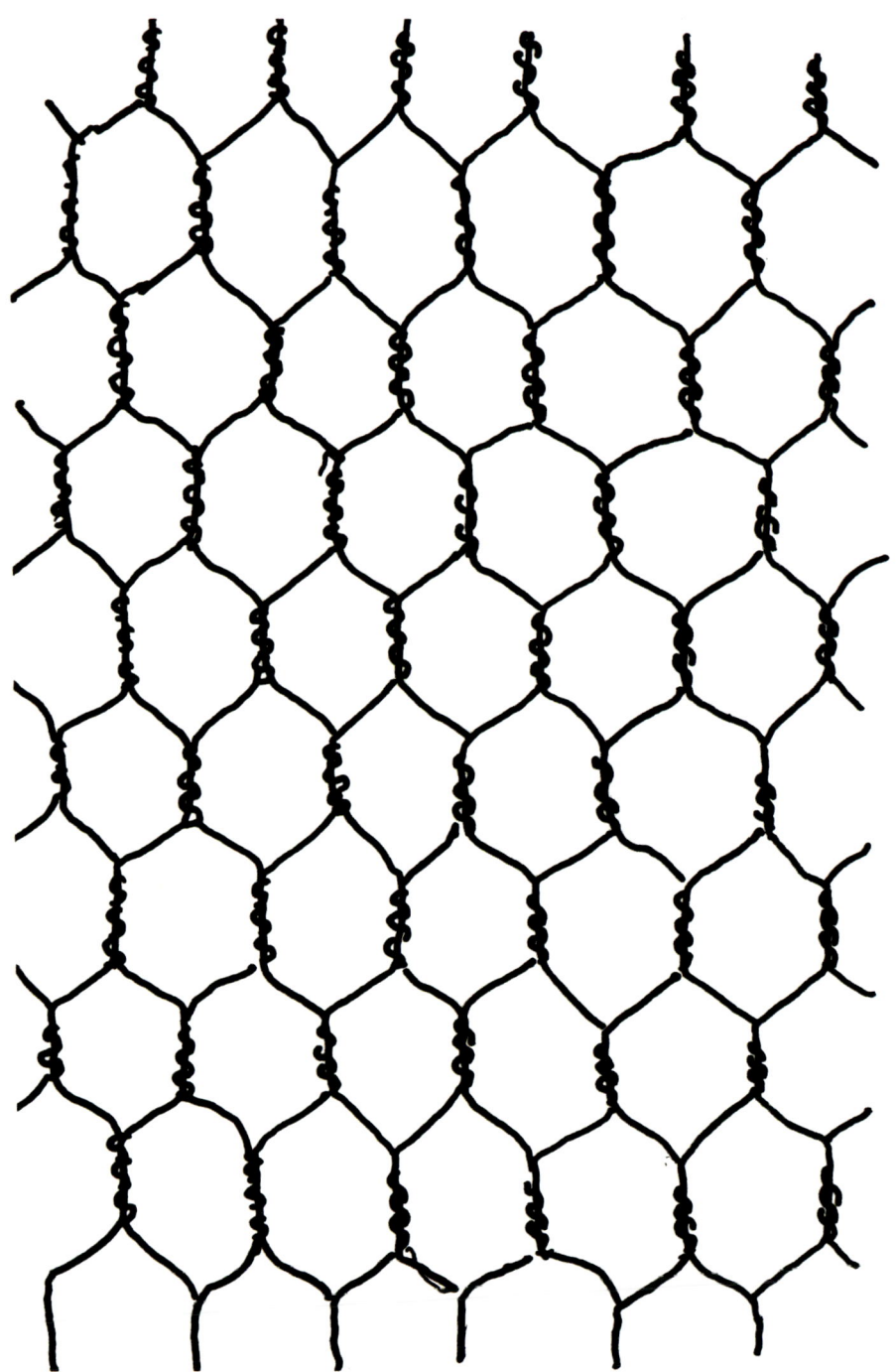

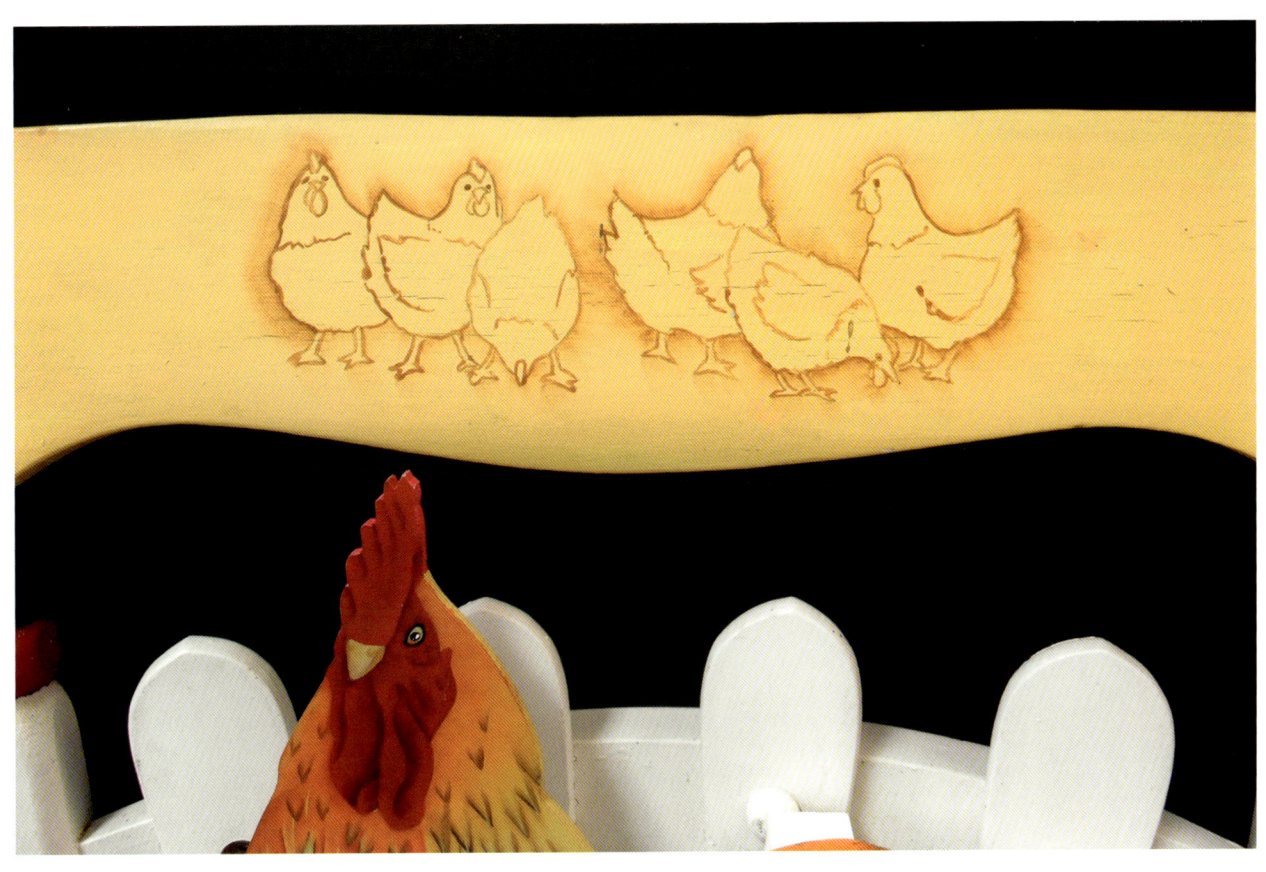

Rooster chair back

Palette — DecoArt

Hi-lite Flesh
Pink Chiffon
Peony
Winter Blue
Uniform Blue
Napa Red
Orchid
Boysenberry
Empire Gold
Raw Sienna
Opaque Yellow
Pineapple
Titanium White

Traditions Paints

Permanent Alizarin Crimson (PAC)
Dioazine Purple
Chrome Green Hue
Teal Green
Blue Green Light
Light Violet

Brushes — Loew-Cornell

Series 7000 # 4 round
Series 7300 # 12 flat
Series 7350 10/0 liner
Series 7550 1" wash

Supplies

Thrift store chair
Tracing paper
Transfer paper
Gum eraser
Scotch tape
Ruler
1/4" Masonite
Sandpaper
White spray paint
Gloss spray varnish
Staple gun
craft saw

ROSE chair

Preparing the Chair

1. Make any needed repairs.

2. Spray paint the chair White.

3. Cut the large rose from the Masonite and sand any rough edges.

Painting the Design

1. Find and mark center on the chair seat. Tape 1-1/2" stripe down the center. Measure and mark 1" stripes, alternating with the 1-1/2" stripes. The narrower ones will be pink.

2. Apply the rose and daisy pattern on the corner of the seat.

3. Paint a 1" border around the seat using a mix of Boysenberry and Napa Red 4:1.

4. Paint the stripes with a mix of Hi-lite Flesh, Pink Chiffon, and Peony 2:2:1; remove the tape.

5. Paint the rose Permanent Alizarin Crimson.

6. Shade it with PAC & Dioxazine Purple 6:1.

7. Hi-light with a mix of PAC and Light Violet 1:1.

8. Use the round brush and Titanium White to paint the daisies.

9. Shade with a mix of Winter Blue and Uniform Blue 2:1.

10. Paint the centers Marigold and shade with Raw Sienna.

11. Hi-lite with a mix of Permanent Yellow and Pineapple 2:1.

12. Where the daisies cross the white stripes, shade with the blue mix.

13. Where they cross the pink stripes, shade with Boysenberry mix.

14. Where they cross the darker border, shade with a mix of Napa Red & Orchid 2:1.

15. Paint the large rose the same way you did the smaller rose.

16. The leaves are based with Chrome Green Hue.

17. Shade with Teal Green.

18. Hi-lite with Blue Green Light.

Finishing Touches

1. Finish with several light coats of gloss spray varnish.

2. Mount the large rose on the back of the chair using a staple gun.

Rose chair back

Rose chair seat

Palette — DecoArt

- Black
- White
- True Red
- Emperor's Gold
- Burnt Sienna
- Shading Flesh
- Hi-lite Flesh
- Antique Maroon
- Antique Rose
- Deep Midnight
- Raw Sienna
- Deep Burgundy
- Medium Flesh
- Winter Blue
- Tangerine
- Neutral Grey

Brushes — Loew-Cornell

- Series 7000 # 6 round
- Series 7300 # 12 flat
- Series 7320 ½" filbert rake
- Series 7350 10/0 liner
- Series 7550 1" wash
- #275 1/2" mop

Supplies

- Thrift store chair
- Blending gel
- Gloss spray varnish
- 1/4" plywood or Masonite
- Craft saw
- White spray paint
- Sandpaper

Preparing the Chair

1. Make any needed repairs and spray paint the chair White.
2. Apply the pattern outline to the plywood and cut out the three pieces.
3. Sand any rough edges.

Painting the Design

1. Apply the pattern and basecoat the face Medium Flesh.
2. Paint the hair and fur Neutral Grey.
3. Paint the suit True Red.
4. Paint the boots and belt Black.
5. Float Deep Burgundy under the beard, the cuffs, down each side of the fur, down the front of the jacket, and above the fur on the pants legs.

Santa's Face:

1. Fill in the eyes solid with White. This helps you to see if they are level, even, and the same size.
2. The irises are Winter Blue with Black pupils.
3. Use the liner brush to outline the irises with Deep Midnight and to pull thin lines radiating from the pupils.
4. Float Deep Midnight around the pupils fading outward.
5. Use the #12 flat to float a faint Black shadow across the eye under the lid fading down and then use the liner to pull a thin line across the edge of the lid. There are no lashes.
6. Place a White comma stroke and dot in each eye for hi-lite.
7. Use Shading Flesh and the #12 flat to shade under the brow and down each side of the nose, across the eyelid, and in the creases at the corner of the eye.
8. Use the same brush and Hi-lite Flesh to highlight.
9. Fill in the mouth with Antique Maroon and paint the tongue Shading Flesh.
10. Shade the lower lip with Shading Flesh and highlight it with Hi-lite Flesh.
11. Apply blending gel to the cheeks and use the wash brush to float Antique Rose across the whole area, skipping the nose. Use the mop to blend and soften.
12. Use the filbert rake and White to overpaint the eyebrows, hair, moustache, and beard. Use the liner brush to get into tight places and to pull stray hairs and curls
13. Use the wash brush and White to wash all white areas.

Santa's Suit:

1. Use the filbert rake to paint the fur and then wash it with White.
2. Highlight the shoulders and sleeves with Tangerine.
3. Shade the suit with Deep Burgundy.
4. Underpaint the buckle and bells with Raw Sienna and then Emperor's Gold.
5. Finish the bells with a Raw Sienna shade and Black holes.
6. Highlight the boots with Neutral Grey.
7. Use the liner and Neutral Grey to make the laces.

Flip pattern for other leg

Santa chair back

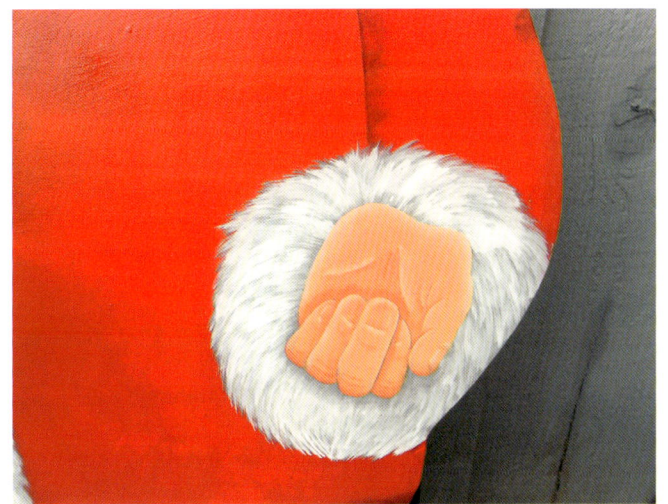
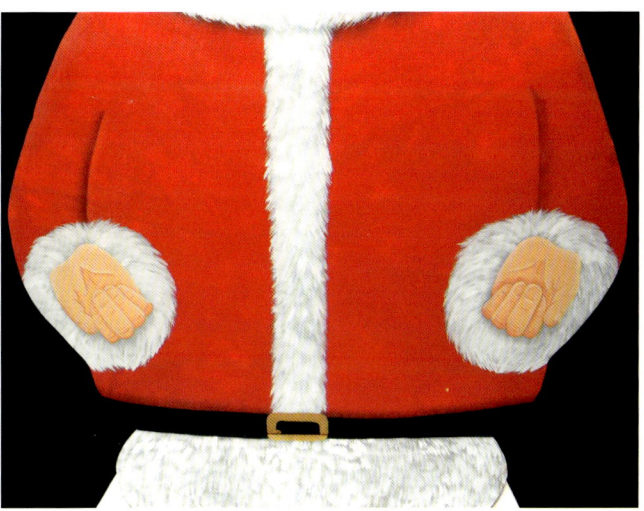

Santa chair seat
Enlarge to fit your chair

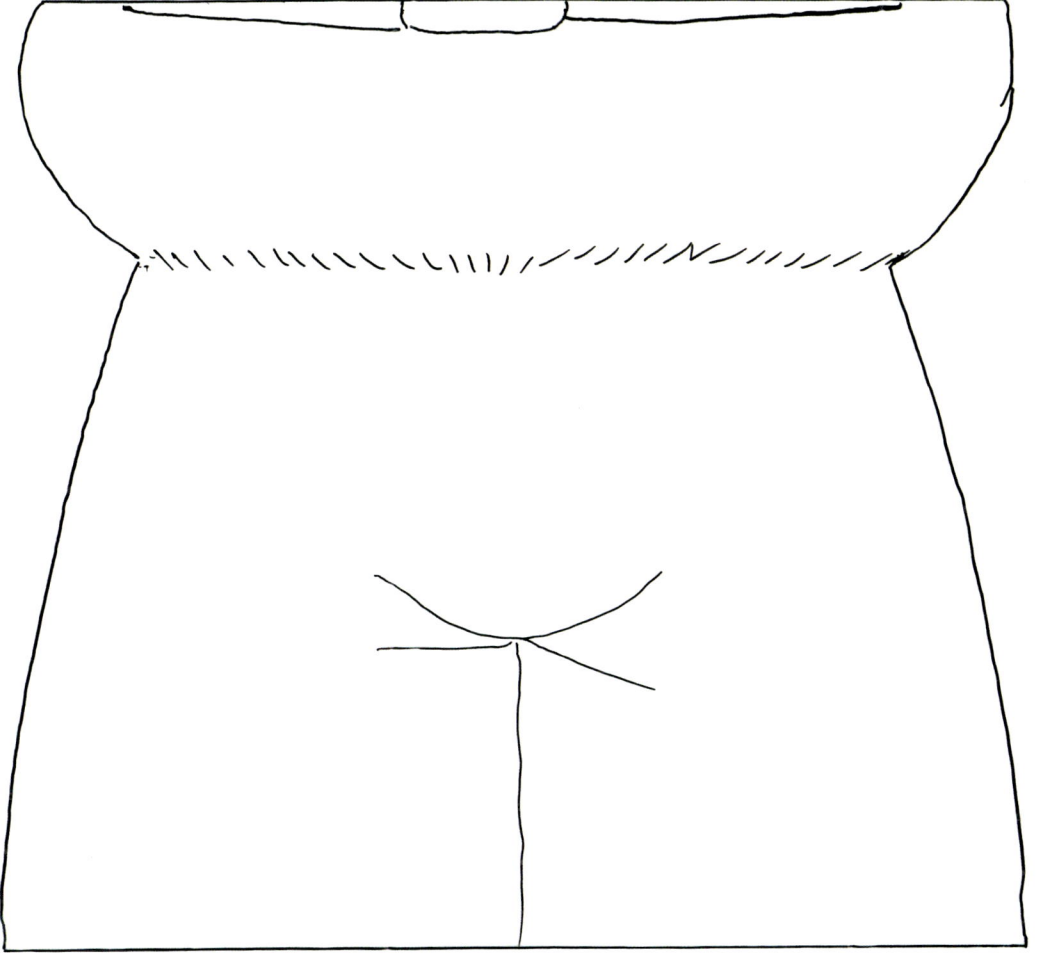

Palette — DecoArt

Hauser Light Green
Hauser Medium Green
Hauser Dark Green
Soft Lilac
Marigold
Raw Sienna
Lemonade
Traditional Burnt Sienna
Dark Chocolate
Asphaltum

Brushes — Loew-Cornell

Series 7300 # 12 flat
Series 7350 10/0 liner
Series 7550 3/4" wash
Series 7850 1/2" deerfoot

Supplies

Thrift store chair
Scotch tape
3/16" Masonite
Craft Saw
Sandpaper
White spray paint
Ruler
Gloss spray varnish
Blending gel

SUNFLOWER chair

Preparing the Chair

1. Cut the large sunflower from the Masonite and sand any rough edges.

2. Spray-paint the flower and the chair White.

Painting the Design

1. Use the wash brush to paint both sides of the flower cut-out Marigold.

2. Paint a 1" border around the seat with Hauser Light Green.

3. Apply the smaller flower pattern to the seat and mark off 1" squares.

4. Paint every other square Soft Lilac.

5. Paint the leaf Hauser Medium Green, shade with Hauser Dark Green, and highlight with Hauser Light Green.

6. Shade both flowers with Raw Sienna and use Asphaltum to deepen some shadows.

7. Hi-Lite with Lemonade.

8. Use the deerfoot and a mix of Dark Chocolate and Traditional Burnt Sienna 2:1 for the centers.

9. Shade the centers with Asphaltum and stipple Hauser Light Green lightly for highlight.

Palette — DecoArt

- Tangerine
- Pineapple
- Cadmium Orange
- Buttermilk
- Oxblood
- Crimson Tide
- Dark Chocolate
- Black
- Hauser Light Green
- Hauser Medium Green
- White
- Hauser Dark Green

Brushes — Loew-Cornell

- Series 7300 # 12 flat
- Series 7350 10/0 liner
- Series 7550 ¾" wash

Supplies

- Thrift store chair
- Ruler
- Scotch tape
- 1/4" Masonite
- Craft saw
- Sandpaper
- White spray-paint
- Gloss spray varnish

TIGER LILY chair

Preparing the Chair

1. Make any necessary repairs to the chair and spray paint it white.

2. Cut the large lily out of Masonite and sand any rough edges.

Painting the Design

1. Mark off 1-1/2" diamonds on the top rail of the back, tape and paint Black.

2. Mark of 1-1/2" border around the edge of the seat, apply the pattern, and mark off 1-1/2" diamonds on the whole seat; paint Black.

3. Use the wash brush to basecoat both sides of the cut-out Lily White.

4. Apply the pattern and base the leaves with HMG.

5. Base the lilies with a mix of Tangerine and Pineapple 2:1.

6. Shade the leaves with HDG and hi-lite with HLG.

7. Shade the lilies With Cadmium Orange.

8. Reinforce deeper shadows with a mix of Oxblood and Crimson Tide 2:1.

9. Hi-lite with Buttermilk.

10. The stamens are Buttermilk with Dark Chocolate ends.

Tiger Lily chair seat

Tiger Lily chair back